Matters of Life and Death

Mark d'Arbon

Matters of Life and Death

To Lloyd
(1949–2021)

60 years is only a long time
at the beginning

Lloyd Stear
Image selected by the Stear family

Matters of Life and Death
ISBN 978 1 76109 663 1
Copyright © text Mark d'Arbon 2024
Cover photos: Barbara d'Arbon

First published 2023 by
Ginninderra Press
PO Box 3461 Port Adelaide 5015
www.ginninderrapress.com.au

Contents

Barbara	9
Gone but not forgotten	
To my friend Lloyd	11
Father and Son	15
Mother and Son	17
My Mother-in-law's Funeral	19
Poem For Jennifer	20
Amy	22
Once More	23
Vale Les Murray	24
Life Goes On	
The Scar	27
Ricardo	29
Seventy Shmeventy	31
Some Birthday Words	33
The Skull	34
It Pays to Advertise	35
Age comes upon us suddenly	38
Body Parts #1	39
I like to dance	41
On Age	42
On Painting the Deck	43
Nightmare	44
Metadreaming	45
Did I Forget Something?	47
The BIG Question	48
From the Corner of Your Eye	50
Night Nurse	52
A Wedding Blanket	53

Pelicans	54
Despair or Reality	55
Getting On My Wick	56
Politics, such as it is	57
The Thing Is	58
Bank	59
the plutocrat	61
Stepping up to the Plate	63
The Governance Creed™	64
Heatwave	69
Oh the Unprecedence	70
Isolationism	73
The Apocalypse	74
Endangered species	76
Protest	78
No aftermath	79
An Uncloudy Day	80
Perspectives	81
Spring Onslaught	82
There's this about the Arctic:	84
Glaciers	85
Winter house	86
Bali Nights	87
A Cameo	88
Gerroa Point 1964	89
Five hundred and fifty years of surfing history	90
A Surfer's Breakfast	92
An Unexpected Upside	93
Brush Turkey	94
In Praise of the Cocktail Frankfurt	95
Second Coming	97
Windows and Doors	98

Ode to an Armpit	99
Sounds	100
Traces	101
View From the Belfry	102
A Poem About the Equinox	103
At Last, the Postmodern Reality	104
Uncertainly Yours	105

It occurs to me
that I am now one of those
I used to call old

Barbara

Love is a renewable resource
Because
Each time I see you
I am replenished.
An anniversary is a snapshot;
A film scene
You, the main character as well as
Plot, setting and support
Over decades,
Making you a timeless hit
For this audience.

Gone but not forgotten

To my friend Lloyd

for Ingrid, Monika and Nick

You wouldn't credit it, Herb*
What a memory
first day in first year
naively proud of a uniform
that symbolised
elitism
orthodoxy
obedience

silly me
I thought that I was special
in some important but ineffable
fashion
until I realised my information
was in error and I cried

you arrived
showed me where to go what to do
became a friend behind enemy lines

throughout those parlous times
we remained a union
sharing a sense of humour
at times macabre and biting
exclusive
since many didn't see the funny side

* A phrase we often used when the unexpected occurred.

Over decades
and decades
we came to know each other very well
knew that the world was a tragic farce
which translated into a rich satire that explained it
very well

I was amazed from time to time
at your effrontery in parlous circumstance
at how you talked yourself in and out of
of trouble with an insouciance
that only once earned you
a punch in the mouth
well you said If that's your level of debate
and walked away
leaving your pugnacious opponent flummoxed

A closed universe of understanding
may have seemed exclusive
containing as it did a lexicon
and imagery that self-referenced
and grew to a word or phrase
containing as many levels as a layer cake
So I suppose it was

But it embraced those close to us
and when a loved one said
give it a rest we did

And speaking of love
I know how well you loved
your children and grandchildren
you spoke of them often
and with gentleness and pride
that gave depth to your humanity

Nothing after you said
you old atheist you
but you're wrong, you know
You live vibrantly
sceptic that you are
In the rich memories
of those who know you well

Platitudes Incorporated would send a card
with all those things that people mouth
on occasions such as this
but there is nothing that can express
the ineffable privilege of
loving you

Father and Son

A photograph
can be at times
more than
a memory
as this one
long forgotten
found in an idle moment

I don't remember
this quiet companionship
but I'm grateful
that we had it

my father was difficult
needing distance
quick to feel slighted
intolerant of difference
and full of anger

every now and then
he could be wise
and surprisingly
sympathetic

this must have been
one of those times

Mother and Son

My mother was Jewish
without ever admitting it
her sons were the apples
of her eye
could do no wrong
she kept all the evidence
of our lives
and when we'd go away
for a time she was
inconsolable
but swallowed it
so her boys
didn't feel guilty
a proto-feminist
to my father's chagrin
she worked full-time
and when he died
she became well-travelled
but still, when I was
an academic and walked
in the formal procession
she took photos of me
as my daughter said
playing dress ups
with my little friends

A photo such as this
and I find myself
missing her

My Mother-in-law's Funeral

Will you take the weight, gentlemen,
He said in a brogue as soft as Irish heather
As we moved the coffin from the hearse.

It was not a heavy lift, as age had shed her bones
Of weight and the coffin merely wood.
So we took the weight easily, sad as it was.

Death is not so bad if it comes in sleep
After a life long and rich with family.
Adventurous, coloured by good friends,
Laughter and an ability to drink all comers
Under the table.

We took her graveside
And placed her gently down,
To be attended by others
After a last farewell.

Memories are not buried with her
Her liveliness and humour stays
To be viewed at leisure.
Reminiscences shared by those of us
To whom she was an excellent friend
As well as a mother-in-law and mother
And so on.

We took the weight.
It was not as heavy
As a last farewell.

Poem For Jennifer

When she laughed
It was as though she
Inhaled happiness
Then guffawed it to
Anyone who listened

the laugh is memorable
It held the essence
Of a life lived fully
Expansively
And kindly

An acreage just enough
For her green thumbs
A garden whisperer
The result a sympathy
with the natural world

Jennifer's farewell was hard
You think
Unjust
And undeserved

But perhaps not so
Fate is just imagination personified
And provides a target for our
Outrage and frustration

It seems that Jennifer knew
That it was time
And so her remnant left
This was not a long goodbye
Her bags were packed long before
Her body stopped

So pause a little
Take a breath and think
Such a short time this was
In a life well lived
So many years
So much done
So much contributed
And distributed

So many friends

The essence of Jennifer is with us
She is not dead
to the memories we have
of this remarkable woman

Amy

Of another age, though well-aged
Where adversity was challenged and
Defeated by a will indomitable.
And virtue was a given, so that
Communities like Batlow thrived
Through Amy and those like her.

The knit and purl of life was in her hands;
The leavening of manners in a naughty world
And the comfort of the table to soothe
The sadness of dreams as yet unrealised.

So Amy leaves us, not to grieve but
To remember and be comforted,
As she would have wished
And later, perhaps over warm scones
And tea in a pot, to reminisce.

Once More

Another uncle bites the dust
None left, on my last count;
Unless there are a couple
Of whom I am ignorant
And vice versa, perhaps.
People die more frequently
Relations or others –
In particular those who are
About my age or just a little
Older…
The end of the runway,
As an old bomber pilot said
Is getting closer, V1 is long gone
Vr has passed
And V2 is inevitable
Sooner rather than later.
A nice metaphor;
Life as an aeroplane
On the runway of time.
And I can see its ending
Not so far away now.
V1? Hmm.

The question, I suppose, is

Where is Air Traffic Control?

Vale Les Murray

I met Les Murray once
Years ago
And he looked
Ordinary
As someone you might meet
Working behind a desk
A senior clerk, perhaps
What a contrast
The man and the mind
Genius wrapped in brown paper
He died, not so long ago
so mourn him as a man
with all his failures and successes
as a man
but not the poet
whose words and rhythms
scintillate with a brilliance of perception
that grasps the humanity of us all

celebrate the powerful grasp of an imagination
that transcends death and makes this poet
immortal.

Life Goes On

The Scar

for George

When I was a young man,
The doctor said,
I was interested in alternatives
Arty-crafty stuff, you know.
Embroidery took my fancy,
Developing as it did
Coordination
Hand-eye efficiency
Fine-motor stuff.
Good for surgery,
As you can appreciate.
I became very good at
Still-life – fruit and flowers
Vases and such.
I still dabble a little, now and then.
That's why, he said, leaning forward
Your scar looks like a daffodil.

Ricardo

what must it be like
living as you do in the depths of the Park
surrounded by bush and a ghost town
attacked from within by the creeping sickness
what must it be like

are your memories friends
or enemies

the mountains climbed
oceans conquered
people from the past
the famous and the infamous

the artist in you
still expressive
I've seen your work
multi-talented, you

we have talked and talked
you the student all those years ago
an incisive mind moderated by
bitter experience
yet still compassionate
today, we share a table
drink coffee and eat experiences
I look forward to each time.

a student-friend and counsellor
many age but few gain wisdom
one of the few, you
you fight and fight
when others throw in a towel
hospital must seem at times
a foyer of hell

I understand Rick
Ricardo
and am amazed
one of the few, you

Seventy Shmeventy

written at the time for Robert

So much is written
About being old as if
It should be avoided:
Boozy Dylan not going gently;
Demented Veronica laughing at those
Who steal her clothes,
Kingsley the pessimist who observed
The brown trees and the run-down wheels –
Not forgetting Oscar and the Picture.

But that was then,
All of them
Memento mori.
Blow that for
A game of conkers, I say!
Today is life and living
Experienced well and truly.
Being able to say
Listen, lad I was doing things –
Important things
Before your father's eye gleamed.

We sang along in days gone
Hope I die before I get old
With Roger;
Demonstrating the ignorance of youth.
Now, we know the benefits of age,
The superiority of cunning
Developed through years of
Fighting the good fight
And banging our heads against a wall
Of brick.

If Faust was a bit more experienced
He would have had more than
Twenty-four years and nothing to show
For the price of his soul.
Maybe the pets are dead, as Brel says,
Le chat est mort mon vieil ami.
But that is not us who still live;
In dog years at least four hundred and ninety –
Not bad at all…
And still plenty more
Where that came from.

Enjoy the taste of life!
A birthday should be a celebration
Not just of survival
But of a knowledge that
At least some of those bastards
Who made life a misery
Are dead.

Some Birthday Words

written for Jean's 60th

Our lives are measured by words
From which we make meaning
And sculpt a world for good or ill
Word lines connect and tie
With others, making fast friends

And lovers

Love-knots of language measure time
And our particular genres and registers
Meld with those of our closest
Evolving into a universe of idiom
That sustains us through the darkness
And provides a lustre that like bright suns
Excludes the shadows of the looming emptiness

Six decades of a gentle life
Tied with the love-knots of a linguist's wisdom
Bind together friends and lovers
And make the world and all its words
For those touched by your idiom
A kinder place.

The Skull

In nineteen seventy-one I marched in solidarity
A city street with jeerers and sneerers on either side
Ahead, the wallopers ready to wallop
A uniformed representation of the military-industrial complex
They did not stay us from the task to end war, bring peace and
Goodwill
But then the cry
The Skull! The Skull's coming!
And the once solidarity of intention splintered into small survival cells
And there he was, head bare as a tiger's claw
Teeth showing in a wolf-grin
Arms apelike
Invisible as a ghost to the serried ranks of police
Who looked fixedly at space, like rabbits in the headlight's glare
The Skull
An animal in almost human form

The last time I saw The Skull
Was at Hurstville station
He was old and bent
No feral strength
No fear
Just age and
Debilitation
But his eyes
Had not changed

It Pays to Advertise

Goebbels was nasty
There's no doubt about that
But he knew how to make people
Believe things
Then
Do things
This evil little man
Is with us still

If he had been born after the war (number two)
He probably would have been
Very successful
In advertising

Here's what he perfected
Repetition
Say it with panache and machismo
Over and over
To an audience that has your attention

Find a scapegoat
Make them responsible
For a problem that
Makes housing out of reach
Prices going up
Jobs being stolen by
THEM

Write speeches for leaders that include
Many ways of avoiding responsibility
Shifting the blame
And make the facile and mundane
Seem important so that
The truth is so disguised that
It doesn't need a bushel to hide under

Oh he was very, very good at
The evil that he did
And it goes to show that
Intelligence without morality
Is as dangerous as poison in a teacup

But the important thing is
About Goebbels and his
Nineteen principles of propaganda
(count them)
That if you know them you can see them
In all their iterations
But importantly
No vitally
In the politics of the polity
The confidence of the confidence man
The sincerity of the long sting
The backslapping baby-holding
How-good-is-thising
And all the other trappings
Of lazy leadershipping
That framed Goebbel's thinking

So be aware that Goebbels was
The maddest of mad men
And do be on the lookout
For evidence that he is still with us
In spirit

Age comes upon us suddenly

leaving us amazed that time has past
the mirrored morning face
returns our stare

My life story etched in the lines
and drooping curves of time's chisel
I'm reminded of the limerick

> *my face I don't mind it*
> *because I'm behind it*
> *it's the people in front that I jar*

Humour moderates age
though the smile droops
occasionally – gravity is not my friend
as yet I eschew trackpants and cardigan
or scrabbling in a purse for change
at the checkout to impatient sighs
although the temptation is there

Pratchett said that inside every old person
there's a young person wondering
what the hell happened
not so me I'm young yet and will remain so
until the trackpants

Body Parts #1

My feet, I thought, were my friends
Over textures rough and smooth
Fast and slow
And in between

My feet
My friends

With me out of the water and in
Confidently carrying me
As I walked
And turned and twisted
On the longboard

And making me look good
As I jogged
Nonchalantly
Back to the car
After a great session
In the waves

And all this for free
No charge
I thought

But I didn't know
That this was a deferred payment plan
Instalments beginning on my sixtieth
And continuing until – who knows?

So now I use them sparingly,
These feet which
I thought
Were my friends
But as it turns out
Probably not.

I like to dance

when no one's home
throw my arms around
boogey down the hallway
tap dance on the tiles
in the bathroom
where the acoustics
add to the performance
me and Bojangles
he slips me a smile
spins around and softshoes
to the lounge room
where Fred Astaire tips his hat
and off we go
tippety tap tippety tap
tappety   tappety   tappety   tip
the tippety tappety trio
Bill and Fred and me
nobody knows
my twinkletoes
'cept Bill and Fred and me

On Age

Few of us – a very few
Survive the ravages of age intact
It's in the bones and flesh
And all the ribbony, twisty bits
That hold our outward shape.
We gravitate towards our feet,
Connected as they are
To that which we
Inevitably return.
A few of us – a very few
Transcend the downward trend
Because the spirit that makes us who we are
Maintains its youth;
So that through our fleshly age
(That makes us what we are)
It retains all those dreams and hopes
That fired us when we were young.
But add to that experience,
Upon which a few – a very few, ponder,
And then transform into something ineffable,
But let's name it wisdom
Then age becomes contained within the parentheses
Of the peripheral
And because of this, those few –
Those very few –
Live forever.
And those who know them –
Call them friends or lovers –
Are much the better for it.

On Painting the Deck

I love boats
all shapes
all sizes
yachts and powerboats
and the boatwords
shearline clinker ketch
leeward windward astern
for'ard and aft port and starboard

I'd like a boat with a fo'c'sle
ketch rigged perhaps
with sheets and cleats and halyards
battens and hatches
gunwales for the swell abeam
a boom vang – there's a phrase
to put the wind in your teeth

bear away and tack or gybe
heel and run the gunnels under
come about to run downwind
away from a lee shore
in force eight on the Beaufort
oilskins soaked with spray
sou'wester flapping in the gale

until then the only deck I'll pace
is the one out the back at home
which I have just painted

Nightmare

Last night I woke
Without an 'I'
No thought
No word
No deed
Last night I woke
And for a second
Or an eternity
All there was
Was time.
No sense
No presence or prescience
No body.
Last night I woke
Afraid
Until I found myself
Aware, awake
Wonderfully

Metadreaming

Reality is a slippery sucker,
Mediated as it is by a chancy old brain,
Where, somewhere, a mind lurks
Like a hungry wolf, lean and eager,
Ready to leap out at the rational
And tear it limb from limb
If your guard is even for an instant,
Dropped.
What hope, then, for the sleeping brain,
With its neurons and electrons
Synaptically shuttered,
Force fields at idle and
The Captain's Chair vacant?
Rationality routed and
The physical fluidified,
So that action becomes a feast
Of absurdity, made reasonable
By a meandering mind, now
Sated by its ever so evanescent
Meal of reason.
I wake and recall a wonder of a dream,
And, in excitement, explain to my constant companion,
My spouse of more than forty years,
The journey that we took, from place to magic place,
Visiting castles and canyons, filigreed and fantastic
Travelling across oceans, in a wooden boat with elephants
And strange captains who demanded
Three hundred and fifty thousand dollars over and above
The original price.
(Because the elephants were bigger than he had anticipated).

And how we all had a whip-round (there was a crowd of us)
And filled a cigar box with the extra cash…
Hmm, she said and uhuh, uhuh.
Strangely uninterested in my gripping narrative,
She looked away and, without further comment,
Walked through the bedroom window into a waiting car.
Which proceeded down the street at a rate of knots
And into the lake, raising a snorkel as it disappeared.
Beneath the suddenly stormy surface.
Much as I disappeared
Beneath a welter of confusion
Only to wake in my disturbed and sweaty bed.
You would not believe, I exclaimed to my spouse
Of more than forty years
The dream that I dreamed.
Hmm, she said, uhuh, uhuh.

Did I Forget Something?

In that bleak and latter moment,
When memory takes its first step into the void
Of unknowing, to be piece by bitter piece
Shattered on the hard rocks of neural indifference;
Then sense becomes an intermittent beacon
Flashing through the dark dog-watches
And across the ocean of unbeing.
By its short but brilliant light,
I think and write
Desperate to capture, if only for a short while
My capacities, that leap about like moths around a flame
And burn, one by one, in its unfeeling heat.

My thoughtless acceptance of an integrated me;
Of the novel brilliance of insight and impulse,
Of emotion and logic,
Woven together in a tapestry of such aesthetic power
That it should cause tears and shivers –
Now amazes me, when all such are in short supply.
That mundane miracle of understanding –
Of reason; of action and reaction –
Seems more precious than the greatest thing
That this material world can offer.

So, when the beacon occults, as it does more often,
There is only darkness
And beneath, a confusion as of an unsettled sea
Against an unseen cliff.
My memory, clutching all that I am
Plummets on.

The BIG Question

It's funny, when you think about it,
That no one ever asks the question
Why have schools?

Seriously, that is.

Schools are grand, the government says
For literacy and numeracy
And all those things that make
Our economy great
Schools keep the kids out of our hair
Say the parents (carers or guardians)
So we only have to worry about them
In the holidays
(Of which there are too many…)

Look at a school and here's what you see.
A fence
Signs that say 'Keep Out'
And buildings clustered together.
Inside the fence.
And the Noticeboard
To keep us up to date.
WELL DONE THE NETBALL TEAM!
It might announce,
But never does it state
THERE ARE SOME CHILDREN IN YEAR 3
WHO ARE UNHAPPY

Nor anywhere can it be read
SAM IN YEAR 6
BELIEVES HE IS A FAILURE
(AND SO DO WE)
Or
MR SMITH (YR 4 TEACHER)
IS A BULLY
And not even
ALL THE CHILDREN
LOVE MRS THOMPSON

Nor will it ever signal that
There is some uncertainty
About whether or not
There should be schools.

From the Corner of Your Eye

Have you seen them, in the dusky evening
Shadows against walls, shapes in the park
Have you seen them, in the early dawning
Draped in doorways, shades in bus sheds
Under bridges and in dank laneways
Have you heard them, at the edge of sound
Muttering into their beards, arguing with the unseen –
The unseen but powerful.
Hunched, they wave their arms about
Aarh, they say, yer will, willyer
Bastards, they cry, protecting their heads
And fearfully look about.
Have you watched them, twitching and ticking
Shrugging the shoulders, shaking the head,
Clutching the bits and pieces, plastic bagged
Possessive of that small belonging
That small humanity that says
It's mine.
I am in control of this small stuff,
Though the world is fit to kick me
With its offhand charity
With its eyes-askance ignorance
With its dangerous, dangerous notice
And bury me in the parks and public places
With my clothes all askew,
My hair in crazy clumps.
My mind God knows where.

Images of misery
Pictures of pain
Distended bellies and round, hopeless eyes
Stare at us through the screen.
We leap to help – thank Christ for distance
And difference –
Tick the box, send the cheque,
Help the orphan somewhere else
Ah, to scatter beneficence, like fairy dust on the wind
That blows over our fence, our place and across the sea,
To feel the warm glow, one more saved.
It helps, when we avert our eyes on the way to work

Night Nurse

Behind the raised counter she sits
Head bent – alone;
Sounds magnified by the stillness.
A stirring and rustling;
A faint groan.

In this ward, a private room
Where tonight a patient is dying;
Politely, no fuss, slipping away
As the moon waxes outside the window.
Gone at first light, before the morning shift arrives

Alone she sits behind the raised counter
Her thoughts her own in the stilly watches;
Kept to herself, as death creeps towards the private room.
Used, almost, by now to this ritual
When life at its low ebb
More easily relinquishes its grip
With a last breath, a twitch.

This night nurse keeps her head bent
And does not look up.

A Wedding Blanket

Knitting
(A soul-soother,
Clicking tips in rhythmic mantra)
The blanket for the new-wedded;
In colours of flamboyant label –
Guava, Java, Raffia and Tuscan,
Nature colours with a hint of mystery.
Raffia in Tuscany? Guava in Java?
No matter, as the needles tick and tack;
And square upon square emerges from the
Ordered anarchy of the wool-ball.
Parts of the whole that will find
The bedded two well wrapped
And snug in chilly times.

Pelicans

Three pelicans riding an updraft
For no purpose it seems
But pleasure
Gracefully ponderous
Wings stretched for lift
Beaks forward legs tucked
In formation
I wonder if the reward
For piloting expertise
Is to be reincarnated
As a pelican

Despair or Reality

the rigours of age send me spinning
to the past,
where life possessed a nimbus
that glowed around living

no intimations of mortality
arrested the inhalations of experience
one on one
and the community of friends standing
against lowering authority
emanating from the uniformed obedience
of mainstream non-think
held us united and forever

such as it was, still it sends a spark
when the uninformed
leap in terror against change
seeing only shadows
on the cave wall
they leave their collective powerful mark
to sanctify the xenophobes
and call it government

And I no longer march

Getting On My Wick

What is it, about race? What strange impulse
Colours our thoughts about colour?
Inside all of us, a sense of place,
Even through cement, the land knows us.
But we deny it, modify and change it
Until the beast is tamed (we think).
And those who claim unity with the dangerous earth
Threaten our control (we own, we control).
We are like children in a sandpit, but more dangerous.
And when others say, we are part of your 'ownership'.
We cry, like children, NO. MINE ALONE!
But when the buried bones of past wrong
Are kicked up, angled out, exposed, we say: NOT MINE!
The fault is others', of another day and time;
Ignoring the earth under the sand.
The past is part of us, our historical skin. We can disclaim but not avoid
There is responsibility without fault, like light without heat,
But yet we deny and deny, transfer our fear of difference
To the terrifying rationalisation of 'not us',
Our place-knowing to owning;
And leave understanding and compassion buried like discarded toys
In the sandpit of our ignorance and fear.
And so they lie and so they die.
Deliberate ignorance is unassailable, an impenetrable fortress
Where understanding is a stranger, an alien countenance;
And logic is the wit of fools, who think that reason is as strong as fear.
At times, intolerance must be the weapon wielded
To smash the seamless fortress of intolerance.
And finally lay to rest the past into its coffin of reality;
Perhaps to think a future that is just.

Politics, such as it is

Me, I was an activist and knew
The enemy well
Their names in a list
Bjelke-Petersen, McMahon
Menzies, Bolte and so on

As well as Thatcher and Reagan
To mention just two

And there were the causes
Vietnam, Land Rights, Nuclear Disarmament
And all of that (go Greenpeace)

It's getting harder
These days, to be politically incorrect
Most of the asylums are run
By lunatics

Trump, Johnson, Morrison Kim Jong-Un,
Duterte, Xi Jinping

But wait – there's more
You might ask what's the point
(Although we mustn't forget Putin)

I think the world is a handbasket
And we all know where that ends up

The Thing Is

Politics is worrying
like a flash flood
it takes us by surprise
and throws up unexpected things
like politicians

A politician can be the log
that smashes things as it is swept
by the fierce current of public opinion
focus groups
and public relations teams

Or a whirlpool that drags everything
into its dangerous vortex of charisma
and confidence
beguiling with a trust-me smile
an I-know-how-to-fix things wink
and nod

The detritus is us if we are swept along
by the flow of personality and persuasion
of plausibility and puff-pieces and we become
a part of the damage that is wrought by this
thoughtless flood of superficiality

The stronger currents are below the surface
a power not seen except by its effects
or by the lens of critique
a capacity to ask how and why and who
and vitally
who said to do it and why

Without this
Nothing

Bank

I remember at school
The suited man from the Commonwealth bank
The passbook and the money box
That looked like a tiny bank

We had to say good morning and thought
That he must have been very important
In his suit with his suitcase
He showed us banking things and
How special it was to save money

Such is mythology

The hero becomes a villain
A scammer, grifter, swindler

Cheat

No suit for this character
Give him a panama hat
A trust-me smile
And a whispered
Have I got a deal for you
Even if you're dead

A wink and a nod kind of guy
Who knows how to wring his hands
And say sorry, sorry – really sorry
Some of the lads and girls need
A good talking to

Bit of a problem with the monitoring
And supervising there – fair cop, he says
Starts to pay the money back

Sincerity is marketable so
Let's forget the parable
Of the widow's mite
And find the agency
That can spin like a Catherine wheel
And heigh ho
Away we go

again

the plutocrat

to be a plutocrat is great
power without responsibility
except to my position of power
I am the ultimate in self-reference
what is good for me
is good
what is good for you
is only good if it's good for me
I'm part of the three percent
which I hate
because I want to be part of
the one percent
It's only human to be ambitious
but I'm more ambitious than
the other ninety seven percent
demonstrably
because I have accountants
countless accountants who count
my assets so I don't have to be
accountable
not my department
talk to my p r guy who can explain it all
me I'm not concerned
what's the point of plutocracy
if you wake in the stilly watches of the night
because you have a conscience
my motto is ethics schmethics
I have people to cover that
they can spin what I do like a top
it's great that I own the media

so I can deal with jumped-up
pinko environmental squealers
who complain because they're really
only green with envy
I'm the only environment that I need to deal with
solipsism moves me to tears
it's great to be a plutocrat
it's really great to be a plutocrat
to be a plutocrat is
great

Stepping up to the Plate

Oh to be a CEO, with everyone
Singing from the same hymn-sheet;
And to have conversations
With line managers who are
On board with the innovative
Human resources package,
Ensuring streamlined restructures
Going forwards.
Even though pushing the envelope
Might create a few bumps in the road;
As long as everyone steps up to the plate
And thinks outside the box in the blue sky;
Then there'll be no need to skate on thin ice.
But, if required strategy outcomes
Are seen by team members to be an overreach
And the ball is fumbled,
Then alternative career paths may be discussed.
At the end of the day
An action-oriented focus
Will get the job done,
So let's SUMO!
(Shut up and move on)

The Governance Creed™

The 2008 School of Education Governance structure

Is designed to efficiently
And comprehensively
Facilitate and coordinate
Activities and responsibilities
In Teaching and Learning,
Research Development and Services.
It is to be understood as a representation
Of current arrangements
But also should be seen as dynamic
And open to change
As the new structures

Are evaluated
                        During the year.

The School's work

Within each of these portfolios
Is addressed by a major
Committee,
A number of more specific Teams,
And a Forum which brings together
Team Leaders and the
Respective Deputy Head of School
(See organisational chart
At end of this document).
School Board brings together
The different
Portfolios,
All of which interact
With the

HOS

Who has ultimate responsibility
For decisions.

The structure is designed

To maximise the capacity
Of focused
Teams
To generate proposals
And documentation
As a basis for discussion
And
Decision-making
At other levels of the
Structure.

Simultaneously,

School Executive members,
The School's three major Committees,
And their related

Forums,

Are to provide for Teams
The necessary policy
And contextual information
And clear priorities
That will enable their activity to be

Productive
And
successful

The intent is to enable input from all staff,

Sometimes
Directly and
Sometimes
Through elected Representatives,
While minimising unnecessary repetition
Of discussion details at the various levels.

All staff will have access through key
Committees
And their
BlackBoard sites,
And through School Board meetings,
To the activities and proposals
Of the various

Teams

And

Executive members.

Accountability for quality and progress
Toward the School's
Strategic goals is built into these

Arrangements.

*

There is a curious ambivalent
Rhythm to the Creed
Which is hypnotic.
The eye moves forward,
Left to right;
Left to right
But the mind lags
And it is not until
The words,
Such as they are,
Complete their journey
That the realisation
Dawns, like the sun
On a cloudy day
That emptiness
Is not only contained by
The spaces in between.

Heatwave

Blazing heat-stroked land
dry tongue-lolling air
leaf-drooping gardens
in parched yards
Dog-panting shade
under trees in empty parks
beer-aroma'd public bars
and sweaty armpits

Melting macadam in parking lots
cars shimmering heat hazed
air-conditioned malls
window-shoppers drinking coolness
Smoke-scent from a distant fire
horizoned clouds of empty promise
hot eucalyptus seeps from trees
an incendiary invitation to a match

Child-cries of pleasure in pools
oases of beach lake and river
thronged with multicolours
searing land left for liquid cooling
Nights of fan-noised perspiration
Imagined open-window breeze
As turgid air rotates around the blades
No relief in darkness as stars shine coldly

Mosquitos and flies flavour the sound and feel
of global warming

Oh the Unprecedence

This pandemic
This Covid 19
Is a tragedy
Unforeseen
But then perhaps it could have been

We have seen it all before but still
Who knew that so many would be ill
Or dead

Who to turn to in this parlous time
Ah well, our leaders (such as they are)
Believe they're doing fine
(But cautiously – responsibility is a poisoned chalice)
UNPRECEDENTED
A fanfare word to cover up
The oops of unlearned history
A narrowness of vision
That failed to see the signposts
Plague
Black Death
Bubonic
Spanish, swine and you name it
All sorts of flu
Not to mention SARS and AIDS
Who knew acronyms could be so deadly

But we endure, isolated as we are
Phlegmatic us we stoics
Sit it out and wash and disinfect
Masked to keep out the nasty bug
The medieval miasma that haunts us still
Unless we're old and tucked away
In places where the foul vapours
Unchecked have their wicked way

What changes
Even banks and insurers
Seem kind
And a government conservative as it is
Is suddenly strangely socialist
Oh dear will all the normalcy raise its hand
So we don't forget what a market economy
Looks like
Street sleepers in hotels what next
Refugees released from durance vile
A bridge too far perhaps
Let's not go overboard

A pandemic moves unchecked
No passport or visa required
And in the best invasive tradition
Lands more heavily on the poor
The marginalised the Third World
Like leaves in Autumn they fall
And are buried in long lines that
Are almost geometric but speak volumes

Oh yes America America
God shed his grace on thee
Not brotherhood but pandemic spread
From sea to shining sea
An example of it's just like the fluism
As long as there are firearms who's to argue

So, here's to 2021 the irony I hope
Is not lost in the cacophony of many voices
Drowning the science which is as far as I can see
Is the only farsightedness around this year
Could 2021 be any worse
Hmm

Isolationism

This

Isolation thing

Is doing

My head

In

Staying at two arm's length

Requires at least two bodies

Hmmm and three if you

Consider a

Queue

The Apocalypse

In an environment that threatens,
Be prepared!
When a pandemic rears
Its ugly head
And those around you
Might end up dead;
Focus,
Focus!
What do you need
To survive this terrifying
Virulent event?
Food – yes food a basic need;
And water – or any fluid that
Can soothe the throat
And drown the stress
Of this life-threatening
Worriesomeness.
What else, what will make
Life bearable at least.
Think,
Think hard!
And consider
Toilet paper.
Yes, that's it! Good thinking there;
Dunny rolls should top the list.

Water pours when it's needed
Food in tins will last for years
But toilet paper is a resource
That will not last, unless of course
You warehouse it. Off you go
To the supermarket
There you'll find the shelves are bare
Of bum fodder.
Oh, tragic day when everyone else
Saw the apocalypse coming;
And got there before you.

How prepared will you be, old chum
When the zombies come…

Endangered species

the northern quoll
the far eastern curlew
the mountain pygmy possum
don't change their behaviour because they're
endangered
they keep on keeping on until
there aren't any left to keep on
keeping on

I noticed that at the last election
when global warming
species extinction
sea level rise
overpopulation and
global bullying
can easily send us the way of the
bramble cay mosaic-tailed rat
which has recently become extinct
that male politicians were wearing
suits and ties
and female politicians were
business-suited too
most of them were spruiking
jobs and tax
and fighting about
who could trust who(m)

just keeping on
keeping on
paying lip-service to those things
that might very well lead to
our species extinction
just like
the bramble cay mosaic-tailed rat

Protest

The seventies was my decade of protest
Subverting the military industrial complex
We put a spanner in the means of production
Made the bosses shiver in their Oxfords

Fuelled by outrage we were
One with the workers
And shared a universal ethic

Apartheid   Land rights   Vietnam
Anathema   Forever   Never

Winning the peace
Non-violently
Which was our mistake
A universal ethic
Is no defence
Against the inertia
Of the powerful

No aftermath

Everyone's gone
Everything's gone
the inferno roared
Leapt and danced lunatic jigs
Insane whirling dervishes of flame
Destruction made visible
Physics and chemistry
At their most appalling
And nothing to be done
Nothing to be done
But watch or run
And hope that
Unlike koalas and wombats
Your life runs with you

An Uncloudy Day

A chilly night,
A gibbous moon
Stars spangling
Silence.
Until a magpie heralds

Morning
And a frosty start,
No cloud.
A sun horizon-balanced
A prophecy of a parched day

The road ribboning ahead;
Eroded edges crumbling
Towards an ancient flatness.
Fences divide a land
That knew no such boundaries
Not so long ago.

Paddocks dry and dusty;
Willy-willys dance across them,
Lifting the topsoil and tossing
Bits and pieces of farmers' dreams.
Across a droughty country.
Occasionally, an optimist
On a tractor
Raises clouds of hope
That blow away in the wind.
Obscuring, for a moment only,
The barren vision of an uncloudy day

Perspectives

At dawn, there is a softness to the mountains;
muting the crags and cliffs that
fall precipitously to valleys.
Shadowed and inaccessible.
Mysterious

Panoramas that ache for captured images
on phone or ipad;
or perhaps a retro SLR with many lenses
hanging from a serious obsessive amateur.
Obscured by fog.

A gash of highway cuts this mountain barrier,
leaving a keloid of strip development.
Fast food and boutique antiquities (New Age).
Yet all around nature's energy threatens.
Immolation.

Blue-tinted immensity
reaches out to our primal senses
and leaves us
speechless.

Spring Onslaught

Today I found a weed
A self-effacing weed
Growing modestly behind
A small tree, hiding itself.
I knew at once that spring
Had crept up on me
And begun its relentless attack of growth
With a small insurgency.

Though not unprepared,
I was a little disturbed
That spring knew the meaning
Of infiltration by stealth
Was familiar with guerrilla warfare strategies
And was confident of victory.

After dealing with this small matter
(The only good weed is a dead weed)
I reviewed my defences:
Lawn mower (with mulching attachment)
Motorised whipper-snipper (heavy duty)
Secateurs (with extendable handles)
Weed killer
Insect killer
Rose, tomato, vegetable (general) emulsions
To fight disease sneak attacks
Snail bait

All checked and ready.
So come on, spring
Do your worst
I am prepared!

There's this about the Arctic:

It's cold.
You need to wrap up warm –
Particularly in storms.
There's wind-chill
That makes it colder still.
The ice is sometimes stained
With dirt, but when it's not
Your eyes are strained
To watch its blinding beauty.

The ocean is a greyish-green
So icebergs stand out starkly
Some loom – hill or plateau sized,
But underneath
They're bigger still.
Others bounce about
Like Maltese terriers.
We saw a growler
Shaped like a duck,
And thought about
The quirky humour
Of wind and water.

Glaciers

Glaciers are awesome
Great cliffs of ice.
There is a subtle blueness,
So I'm told;
And glaciers are very old.
We saw a cliff of ice
Fall into the sea.
It roared, in defiance or pain
Hard to tell, but I must say
It made my hair (what's left of it)
stand up; and I gasped
At its stupendous power
I could have surfed the wave
It made, as it thundered
And became an iceberg.
Wow!

Winter house

The cold seeps slowly
oozing slyly under the door
and through uncurtained windows

this room no haven of warmth
no toasty blankets or friendly flames
in a bum to the fire hearth

icicles from the eaves
a chill that catches the throat
but there is no throat here

floorboards shrink and creak
as icy fingers torture edges
twisting the wood relentlessly

stasis of chairs and table
a frozen drop hangs from a tap
cold enough to burn fingers

but none are there for the pain

A frozen silence engulfs each room
until a key click and
a hum of air conditioner
begins to banish winter
for a short time

Bali Nights

Darkness falls like a gentle sigh.
The night air, redolent with exotic scents
Enfolds us: a sarong of the softest silk
A counterpoint of frog and cricket
Accompanied by the susurration of
A breath of breeze.
In the ceiling, a gecko calls its luck

A Cameo

Small temples of mellowed stone
Moss covered
Among paddy fields of serried ranks of rice
New planted
Ducks among them

Sudden valleys of steep beauty
A stream below, water clear and singing
Bathers glistening on the shaded banks
And a nostril tickling scent of mystery.

Gerroa Point 1964

A still morning with the sun
a golden suspicion on the horizon.
From the cliff, watching waves
in clean lines break beside
a deserted rock platform,
glittering with small pools;
reflecting a still and pearly sky.

We can surf that.

No one before us,
no fin had carved an arc
in this break.
Except dolphins, perhaps.
No wave ridden here.

Rock is hard on bare feet
but adrenaline is harder.

Down to the rock platform
a pause to watch
as the swell peels perfectly
to the left.

And so we begin.

The first wave is mine.
A sweet feeling
to be the first.
Not like climbing Everest –
but nonetheless a rush.

Five hundred and fifty years of surfing history

drink coffee at the kiosk
beside the home beach
faces wrinkled like a ruffled ocean
onshore and small so no longboards
in the break or SUPs
so they sup
their coffee and reminisce
old days old ways
spots now famous but not then
south to the Farm Werri and
Green Point
Bermagui
Narooma and Moruya
north to Scotts and Crescent
Angourie Snapper Rocks Byron Burleigh
and NOOSA
places in between names forgotten
but always offshore and four to six foot
these days the home break and nearby
is good enough although
there are the trips Sumatra Bali
Sri Lanka on air-conditioned boats
and other places that decades back
were inaccessible unavailable

such stories are told among the five hundred and fifty years
and all nod and say I remember but what about when
a club of such experience as to boggle the younger mob
surfing as they were before the parents
were a gleam in grandparents' eyes
tomorrow the wind may change
offshore a westerly tinged with autumn
three-to-four-foot swell
standing up nicely
five hundred and fifty years of surfing history
in the break and cruising
coffee later

A Surfer's Breakfast

A loaf of bread
Fresh from the bakery
With the smell of it
Twitching nostrils
Exercising salivary glands
Warm as an ironed sheet on a chilly night
Hot chips, grease engorged
Lots of them wrapped in paper
Absorbing the drips
Butter – the real stuff
Hovering at the melting point
But firm enough
Rip the core of bread out
Leaving a hole surrounded by crust
An implement – perhaps a knife –
A stick will do in a pinch
To slather the butter around
Pour in the chips until the protesting crust
Begins to crack
Flatten it
Pick it up, both hands
Eyes closed
Mouth open to the point of ache
Then bite into this exquisiteness
As the butter and grease
Make your chin shine

An Unexpected Upside

Today, the beach was unpeopled
The kiosk was bare of a queue
A dearth of cars in the carpark
Enhanced a desolate view
This virus pandemically active
Has plenty of downsides, for sure
But, homophonically speaking,
It's great for the state of the shore

Brush Turkey

Brush turkeys feed
on insects and seeds
fallen fruits
raking the leaf litter
breaking open rotten logs
with their large feet.
They obtain food from the ground
usually in somebody's garden
occasionally feeding on ripening fruits
usually in somebody's garden
usually in somebody's
painstakingly maintained
expensively extensively
landscaped and organically balanced
garden
which they deliberately obsessively
vindictively and actively ruin
brush turkeys are protected
under the Biodiversity Act of 1996
but most gardens aren't
I simply ask the question
Is that fair

In Praise of the Cocktail Frankfurt

Not haute cuisine;
Humble,
Red,
The Cocktail Frankfurt
Is much maligned;
Relegated to the children's party
With
Patty cakes
And fairy bread.

And yet
When heated just so
And dipped in sauce
(Red on red)
There is a spiced piquancy
To this entrée
That suits my palate
When I am fed.

The Cocktail Frankfurt!

In miniature
It is, you see
A lovely, sneaky savoury

When others scoff the canapés
With snooty, Francophilic names
I, a lonely connoisseur
From such fripperies demur

My palate craves the cocktail frank
It is the gustatory plank
'Pon which my diet balances
No matter what the gourmet says

Oh! Cocktail Frankfurt let you be
The food that ever pleaseth me!

Second Coming

He stood on the swell in the harbour,
Arms spread, head high.
He called to those in the ferries and skiffs
I have come again
Who will come with me;
To become fishers of men?
One, an angler, heard the call
And stepping overboard
Ran across the water,
Took him by the hand and said
There are some advantages to pollution

Windows and Doors

I wondered long, as in a cloud
Meandering I, through streets and lanes;
Past dwellings, standing small or large
Their doors and windows framed and paned;
And silent – no one seemed in charge
Beyond the fence and garden beds.
I ambled on, inside my head.

Continuous as geometry
These doors and windows firmly shut.
The same in rectangularity
Some with curtains and some not.
Dozens saw I at a glance;
My hands in pockets in my pants

Nor doors nor windows did not dance
Like gleeful daffodils or waves;
Poetic image? Not a chance
In this rectanglish urban maze.
I gazed a bit, then gazed some more
At doors and windows – what a bore.

Now oft, as on my couch I lie
Vacantly pensive, in a mood;
Embedded in my inner eye
Are doors and windows, framed in wood.
And then I rise and get a drink
Sometimes of water, from the sink.

Ode to an Armpit

An armpit is an emptiness defined
By arm and chest in juxtaposed array.
'Though in truth 'tis coarse and unrefined,
When haired and sweated on a humid day.

Yet an armpit cannot stand alone.
When shaved; and scented like a garden plot
It seems that two of them must needs be shown;
Decorative – for the advertising slot.

And so, despite its humble, hidden state
It seems the armpit must become exposed
Else, deodorants would for profit scarcely rate
And lifts would be a torture to the nose.

Sounds

a post-constructivist anti-universal narrative

Closer than the ear can hear
The sound
Arrived as in a dream
Of listening
And yet being in a sense deaf
To another reality
Not known to the listener

So it is that the listening one
Speaks to the orator
Who makes the speech that no one
Can hear because it is below the audibility
Of those who need to hear
The politicians and such as they
Moving and shaking the universe of thought
And action where might becomes not right but
At least just in such a way as justice seen
To be undone, as all are done in or out
Side the third of worlds a fraction too large
To be ignored where such ignorance is bliss
The folly is not in wisdom but the opposite a seemingly
Cyclic coincidence

And Also

Traces

the ghost language
is not for those with ears
or eyes or nose
the ghost language
is traced
by spectral fingers
from the depths of memory
and in the sunless
moonless
starless
darkness that she shares
with the spectres
of the past
and no-one living
such is the ghost language
such is the haunting

But as well:

View From the Belfry

my wings cool in the evening breeze;
perched in the belfry
with the bats and
other nocturnal dreamers
above the church
the graveyard snuggling in beside it
I watch the path and the lychgate
the climbing rose that wends
its way around the struts
and over the roof
A lovely, lively thing
with blossoms and leaves
hiding the thorns beneath
like life and there is father
in the garden petals drooping
down I fly and land
beside him
why so sad my daffodil Dad
I ask and
wriggling his roots
arthritically he sighs and says
Never enough sun Son
Never enough son

A Poem About the Equinox

Balance in all things
Quoth the guru,
I'm unaware of who
He was;
But Wisdom is a universal
Understood by many people.

So, let's celebrate the equinox
A circumstance no one should knock;
Equal parts of day and night,
Seems to get the balance right.

I like the Latin whence it comes
(e.g. *cogito ergo sum*)
aequus (equal) and *nox* (night)
gives us equinox, alright?
It's great to know an ancient script
(a status thing, you get my drift?)
So let's all be equinoctial –
A glass half empty – and half full.

At Last, the Postmodern Reality

Beautiful princess, golden-haired,
Wanders, in the balmy air,
Singing gaily a roundelay,
Gracing a joyous summer's day.
By a rivulet she kneels
To find how cool the water feels.
At her side a small, green frog,
With spotted hide and eyes agog.
On an impulse, frog she grips
And presses it to ruby lips…
Ah, cast away romantic thoughts,
The frog was a toad and she got warts.

Uncertainly Yours

Don't look for certainty
you're doomed to fail
Russell tried it
waste of time

should have called it *Principia Mathamessica*

Euclid thought he had it
but he didn't
Kronecker refused to accept it
and who knows him
which goes to show
you can be bright
and dull at the same

time

alephs zero and one
will do you in
even in an infinite universe

Cantor diced with the infinite
unlike god
and ultimately lost
ending in an asylum
for the infinitely bewildered

think outside the square, an axiom
that makes no sense when your limits
are straight lines of equal length
and right angles

oh and two dimensions

are you depressed to know
that the universe is like a complex square
in many dimensions
and all you can know is at best
what's in it because you are

it's enough to do you in
an infinite number of infinities
all completely different
including value

infinity times one equals infinity
so does infinity times two,
but differently
it fries my brain

but in a good way

don't look for a list of instructions
to find the proof of truth
there is no recipe
David Hilbert found out
after asking twenty-three questions
then big Al Turing found the

uncomputable

refer to Gödel and his excellent
incompleteness theorem
you might understand it
but it's outside my personal universe

quantum don't get me started
Feynman said if you think you understand
quantum mechanics you don't understand
quantum mechanics
I agree and have no constant Planck
which is in si 6.62606×10^{-34} J·s.
on which to stand

the list is not in chronological order
but then neither is time apparently

what confidence we could have if none
of these smart alec mathematicians
and scientists never existed

www.ingramcontent.com/pod-product-compliance
Lightning Source LLC
Chambersburg PA
CBHW071008080526
44587CB00015B/2387